STAR WARS®
WORKBOOKS

2ND GRADE READING

FOR AGES 7–8

BY THE EDITORS OF BRAIN QUEST
CONSULTING EDITOR: MICHAEL FLYNN

WORKMAN PUBLISHING
NEW YORK

Library of Congress Cataloging-in-Publication Data is available.

ISBN: 978-0-7611-7812-5
Workbook series design by Raquel Jaramillo
Cover illustration by Mike Sutfin
Interior illustrations by Scott Cohn

Workman books are available at special discounts when purchased in bulk for premiums and sales promotions
as well as for fund-raising or educational use. Special editions or book excerpts can also be created to specification.
For details, contact the Special Sales Director at the address below, or send an email to specialmarkets@workman.com.

Workman Publishing Co., Inc.
225 Varick Street
New York, NY 10014-4381

workman.com
starwars.com
starwarsworkbooks.com

Printed in the United States of America
First printing June 2014

10 9 8 7 6 5 4 3 2

This workbook belongs to:

_____

Jar Jar Words

Use an **ar** to complete the words that have the same vowel sound as **Jar Jar**. Then say each word out loud.

Jar Jar

 g___den

 p___ty

 y___n

 MagnaGu___ds

D___th Maul

 st___

 f___m

Write all the **ar** words in alphabetical order.

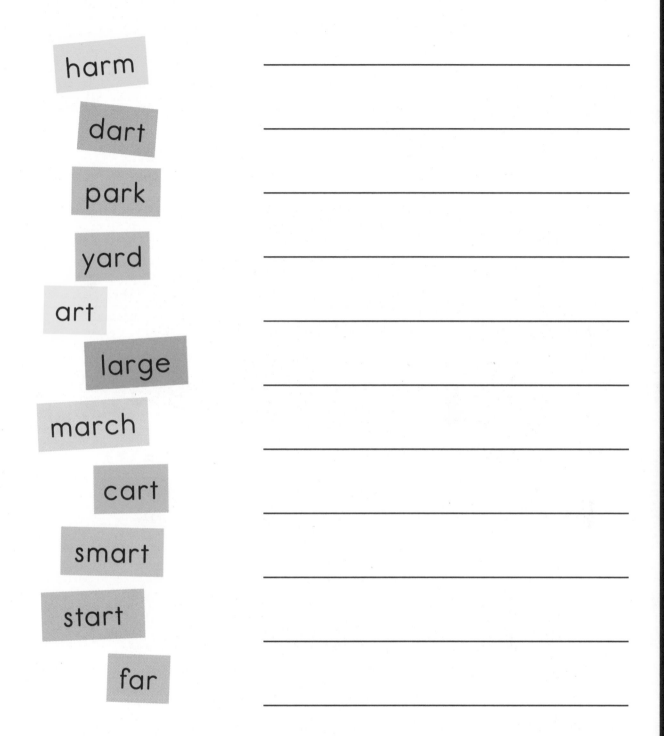

harm

dart

park

yard

art

large

march

cart

smart

start

far

_____

_____

_____

_____

_____

_____

_____

_____

_____

Write a sentence with one or more of the **ar** words on the list.

_____

_____

Your Turn!

Some words have the same vowel sound but are spelled differently.

Say each **ear**, **er**, **ir**, and **ur** word out loud and listen for the vowel sound.

herd

first

third

trooper

purple

purse

research

search

learn

survive

birthday

hurt

shirt

circle

perfect

burn

earth

bird

podracer

universe

Sort the words by spelling pattern in the boxes below.

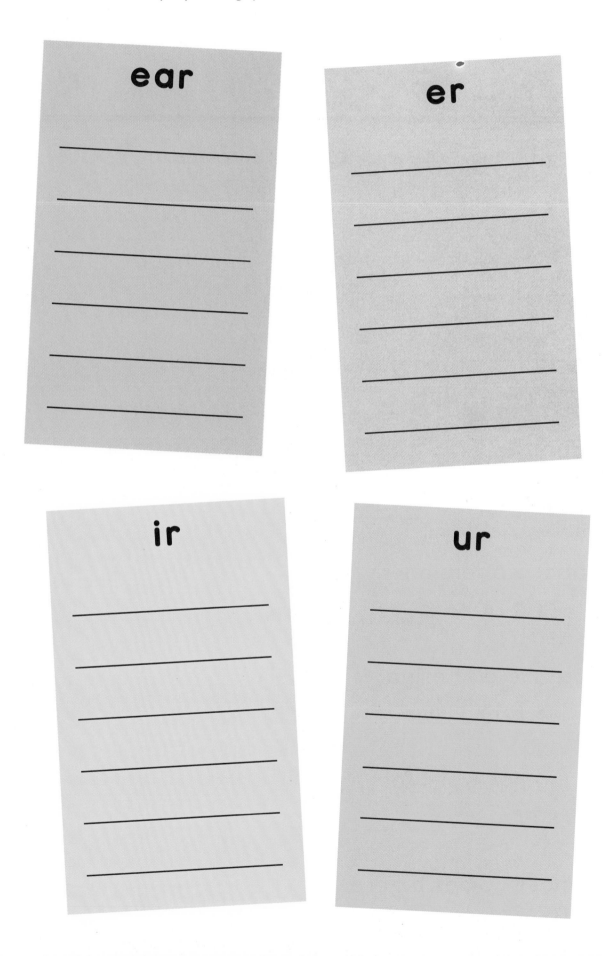

ear

_____

_____

_____

_____

_____

er

_____

_____

_____

_____

_____

ir

_____

_____

_____

_____

_____

ur

_____

_____

_____

_____

_____

Rancor Game

Say each word out loud. Read the clues. Unscramble the words.

horns   more   soar   rancor   floor   orbit   four   roar

Jabba the Hutt has one of these in his palace.

C R O R N A   _ _ _ _ _ _

Saesee Tiin has these coming out of his head.

R H N S O   _ _ _ _ _

Planets do this around a sun.

B T O R I   _ _ _ _ _

The opposite of "less" is this word.

R E O M   _ _ _ _

Chewbacca often makes this sound.

O R A R   _ _ _ _

The opposite of "ceiling" is this.

O L O F R   _ _ _ _ _

This is another word for "fly."

R O A S   _ _ _ _

This number comes before "five."

U O R F   _ _ _ _

All of the words you unscrambled have the same vowel sound as **rancor**, but they are spelled differently.

Sort the words by spelling pattern in the boxes below.

or

_____

_____

_____

oar

_____

_____

oor

_____

_____

_____

ore

_____

_____

our

_____

_____

Find the words you sorted in the word search.

Circle the words you find.

P	R	T	S	O	B	F	T
H	U	S	O	A	R	H	S
O	R	S	F	L	O	O	R
R	O	A	R	A	U	R	U
B	M	O	R	E	R	N	O
I	O	R	O	R	B	S	T
T	R	E	A	F	O	U	R
R	A	N	C	O	R	O	R

Count Down!

Complete the clues with words that have the same vowel sound as **count** or **down**.

Fill in the crossword puzzle using the words you complete.

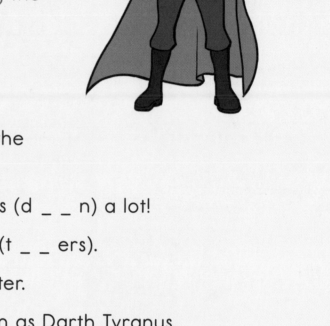

ACROSS

3. There are 12 Jedi who sit on the Jedi High (C _ _ ncil).

4. Jar Jar Binks is clumsy. He falls (d _ _ n) a lot!

5. Coruscant is a city full of tall (t _ _ ers).

6. Boba Fett is a (b _ _ nty) hunter.

9. (C _ _ nt) Dooku is also known as Darth Tyranus.

11. Amidala is a queen but she doesn't wear a (cr _ _ n).

DOWN

1. The opposite of "whisper" is (sh _ _ t).

2. The Force is a (p _ _ erful) energy field.

6. Wookiees have (br _ _ n) fur.

7. You use a (t _ _ el) to get dry.

8. The past tense of "find" is (f _ _ nd).

10. Mos Espa is a (t _ _ n) on Tatooine.

Droids Destroy!

Sort the words by spelling pattern in the boxes below.

droid   boy   point   annoy   toy   choice

voice   royal   destroy   enjoy   boil

join   oil

oi

_____

_____

_____

_____

_____

_____

oy

_____

_____

_____

_____

_____

_____

Look at the Moon!

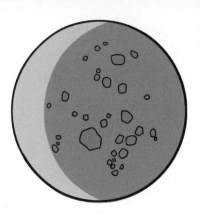

Some **oo** words have the same vowel sound as **look**.

Some **oo** words have the same vowel sound as **moon**.

Sort the words by their **oo** sound in the boxes below.

spoon   tooth   cook   hook   shook   wood

loose   Dooku   balloon   hood   took

Naboo   book   good   soon   Plo Koon

look

_____   _____   _____

_____   _____   _____

_____   _____   _____

moon

_____   _____   _____

_____   _____   _____

Opposites!

Antonyms are words that have opposite meanings.

Read each sentence. Circle the **antonym** of the underlined word in each sentence.

Jango Fett can fly <u>up</u> in the air with his jetpack.

around   down   high

Anakin's podracer is <u>first</u> in the race!

last   second   next

It is so sunny and <u>hot</u> on Tatooine!

warm   bright   cold

Chewbacca is very <u>tall</u>.

furry   short   happy

Mace Windu is a very <u>wise</u> Jedi Master.

dumb   tough   sad

Han Solo says that the *Millennium Falcon* is a <u>fast</u> ship.

speedy   slow   tired

Write a sentence for each of the **antonyms**.

_____

_____

_____

_____

_____

_____

_____

_____

_____

Similars!

Synonyms are words that have similar meanings.

Read each sentence. Circle the **synonym** of the underlined word in each sentence.

Yoda may be the smallest Jedi,

but he is also the most <u>powerful</u>.

happy   weak   strong

C-3PO can <u>speak</u> over six million languages.

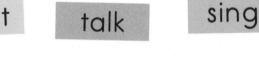

silent   talk   sing

R2-D2 is <u>tiny</u> compared to C-3PO.

big   same   little

Padmé is <u>brave</u> when she battles the nexu.

fearless   scared   sleepy

Many Imperial officers are <u>scared</u> of Darth Vader.

unafraid   frightened   loyal

Chewbacca is Han Solo's <u>best</u> friend.

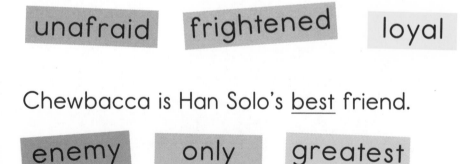

enemy   only   greatest

Write a sentence for each of the **synonyms**.

_____

_____

_____

_____

_____

_____

_____

_____

_____

Night, Knight!

Homophones are words that sound the same but have different spellings and meanings.

Read each sentence. Circle the correct **homophone**.

Luke is a Jedi (Knight) / **Night**.

The **some** / **sum** of three plus three is six.

Tatooine has two **suns** / **sons**.

Princess Leia is on a **peace** / **piece** mission.

No one **guessed** / **guest** that Luke was Leia's brother!

Rancors eat a lot of **meet** / **meat**.

Beru is Luke's **ant** / **aunt**.

Write a sentence for each **homophone** that you did not circle.

_____

_____

_____

_____

_____

_____

_____

_____

_____

_____

Batches of Lightsabers!

Plural means more than one. For most words, add **s** to make a singular noun plural. For words ending in **sh**, **ch**, **tch**, **s**, or **x**, add **es**.

Write the plural for each word by adding **s** or **es**.

lightsaber_____

batch_____

tree_____

box_____

glass_____

bench_____

bush_____

bus_____

Ewok_____

watch_____

stormtrooper_____

ax_____

Weird Plurals!

Some singular nouns do not take **s** or **es** to form plurals. These nouns have **irregular plurals**. An irregular plural changes the spelling of the word.

Draw a line from the noun to its **irregular plural**.

tooth	mice
child	teeth
goose	men
foot	feet
woman	geese
man	people
mouse	children
person	oxen
ox	women

Write each of the **irregular plurals** on the lines below.

_____ _____ _____

_____ _____ _____

_____ _____ _____

Tell Me Something!

A **sentence** is a group of words that expresses a complete thought.

Read each group of words. Underline the complete **sentences**.

Remember, you always begin a sentence with a capital letter and end with a period.

Tusken Raiders live in tents.

The stars in the galaxy.

Luke, Leia, and Han.

Chewbacca can fly the *Millennium Falcon*.

The small, furry Ewok.

C-3PO is very shiny.

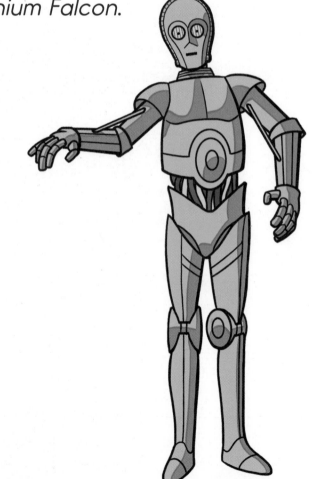

Darth Vader wears a mask.

The droids you're looking for.

It happened a long time ago.

Write a complete **sentence** for each group of words that you did not underline.

Question or Statement?

A **question** is a sentence that asks something.

A **statement** is a sentence that tells what someone or something is doing, or what someone or something is.

Copy each sentence on the line below it.
Add a question mark if the sentence asks a **question**.
Add a period if the sentence is a **statement**.

How many Ewoks do you see

_____

Will Anakin become a Jedi Knight

_____

He wears a black robe

_____

Who is looking for Obi-Wan Kenobi

_____

Will Lando help Han escape

_____

Padmé loves Anakin

_____

Exclamations and Commands!

An **exclamation** is a sentence that shows a strong feeling.

A **command** is a sentence that tells someone to do something.

Copy each **sentence** on the line below it. Add an exclamation point to turn each into an **exclamation** or a **command**.

We need to get out of this asteroid field.

_____

Watch out.

_____

I thought you said this ship was fast.

_____

Go faster.

_____

That asteroid is coming right at us.

_____

We did it.

_____

Spelling Break!

Write each of these spelling words two times.

universe

purpose

choice

clumsy

glass

orbit

watches

learn

floor

royal

captain

circle

axes

asteroid

knife

found

Choose any six of the words. Write a sentence for each one.

_____

_____

_____

_____

_____

_____

_____

_____

_____

Common or Proper?

A **common noun** is a word that refers to a person, place, or thing.
A **proper noun** is a word or group of words that names a specific person, place, or thing.

Underline the **common nouns** in each sentence.
Draw a circle around the **proper nouns**.

(Anakin) uses many different tools to build the droid.

Queen Amidala comes from Naboo.

Both the Jedi and the Sith use lightsabers.

The moons orbit around the planets because of gravity.

Many strange creatures live in the swamps of Dagobah.

Sort all the **nouns** you underlined and circled in the boxes below.
Don't forget to capitalize the proper nouns.

person	place	thing
_____	_____	_____
_____	_____	_____
_____	_____	_____
_____	_____	_____
_____		_____

Pronouns!

A **pronoun** is a word that can take the place of a noun. Read the **pronouns** in the boxes.

Rewrite each sentence with a **pronoun** in place of the underlined word or words.

He   She   It   We   They

<u>Kit Fisto and Plo Koon</u> fight the droids.

<u>They fight the droids.</u>

<u>Aayla</u> joins the battle.

_____

<u>Mace Windu</u> comes to help.

_____

Mace says, "<u>All of us</u> are stronger than they are!"

_____

_____

He quickly destroys <u>a droid</u> with his lightsaber.

_____

_____

Younglings!

The **subject** tells who or what a sentence is about.
The subject can have a **noun** or **pronoun**.

Underline the **subject**. Circle the **noun** in the subject.

The Jedi (Temple) is an exciting place.

Younglings from every part of the galaxy
become Jedi Knights.

Yoda teaches the younglings every day.

The tallest youngling is called Gungi.

Gungi is a Wookiee.

All the younglings train and play together.

If they train hard, they may grow up to be
Jedi Masters like Yoda!

An **adjective** describes a noun.
Color, size, and number words are **adjectives**.

Circle the **noun**. Underline the **adjective** or **adjectives**.

furry (Wookiee)

blue lightsaber

green skin

five brave younglings

big rock

two eyes

Jedi Knights!

A **verb** is an action word. It tells what someone or something does. A **present-tense verb** tells what is happening now.

Use the **action words** below to tell what the Jedi Knights are doing.

fixes   talks   jumps

walks   picks   climbs

Kit Fisto _____ a bantha down the road.

Aayla Secura _____ a flower.

Plo Koon _____ to Bultar Swan about the weather.

Saesee Tiin _____ the droid with his tools.

Luminara Unduli _____ over the puddle.

Shaak Ti _____ up a tower.

A **past-tense verb** tells what happened in the past. You add **ed** to make many verbs **past tense**.

Rewrite each sentence on the previous page in the past tense by changing the verb. Replace the **s** or **es** with **ed**.

_____

_____

_____

_____

_____

_____

_____

_____

_____

The Battle of Geonosis!

Adverbs tell more about a **verb**. **Adverbs** tell **where**, **when**, or **how** something happens.

Underline the **verb** in each sentence. Circle the **adverb**.

Mace Windu and 200 Jedi traveled quickly to Geonosis.

They battled the droids there.

The Jedi bravely fought the enemy droids.

Later, Yoda arrived with thousands of clone troopers.

The Jedi and clone troopers surrounded the droids inside the arena.

Afterward, the Jedi left the planet.

Write each **adverb** you circled in the correct box below.

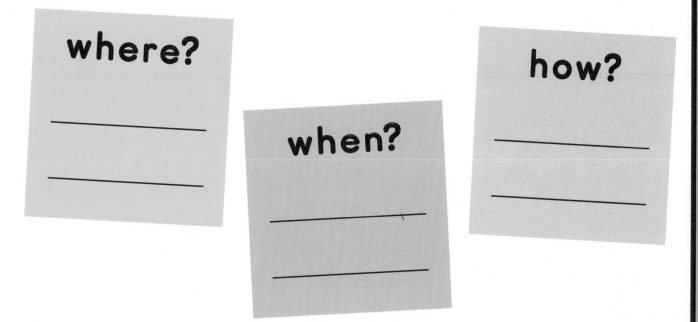

where?

_____

_____

when?

_____

_____

how?

_____

_____

Write a sentence for three of the **adverbs**.

_____

_____

_____

_____

_____

A Poem

Read the **poem**. Then answer the questions.

The Lightsaber

When in the darkest time of night
Impossible can seem the light,
The memory of every sun
Fading, one by one by one.

So easy to forget that hope
Can be the strongest kind of rope
To pull us back upon the course:
And find a way back to the Force.

In Ilum's icy caves of gloom,
Crystals shine like flowers bloom,
The light in them will never fade:
The source of my Jedi blade.

"The Lightsaber" is a **poem** that **rhymes**.

Fill in the boxes with **rhyming words** from the poem. Then add your own **rhyming word** to the lists.

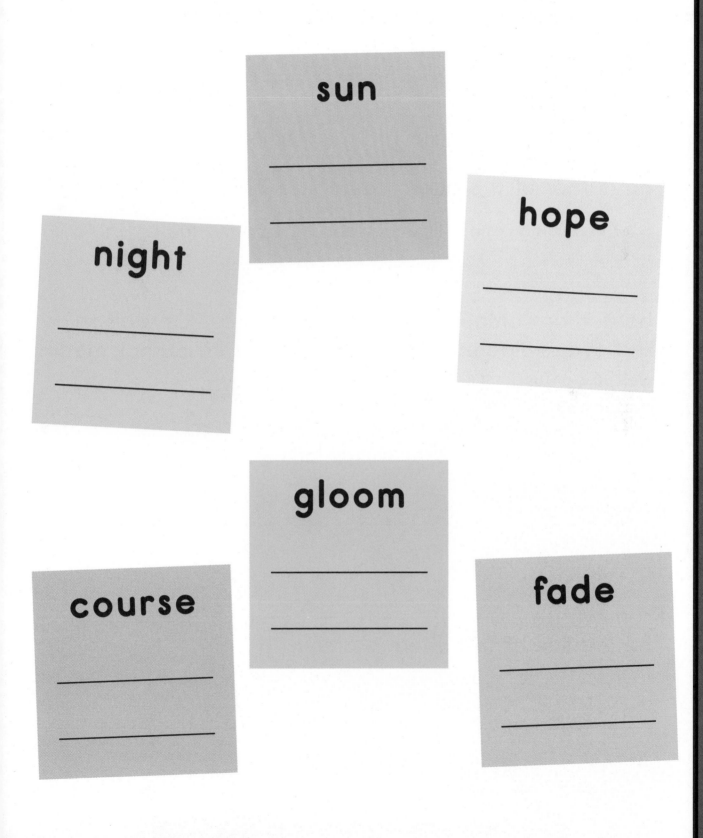

sun

_____

_____

night

_____

_____

hope

_____

_____

gloom

_____

_____

course

_____

_____

fade

_____

_____

Answer the questions about the **poem** "The Lightsaber."

The first line of the poem sets the mood:
"When in the darkest time of night…" Which
word best describes the mood of the poem?

☐ happy   ☐ thoughtful   ☐ silly

The author of the poem compares "hope" to:

☐ a strong rope   ☐ an icy cave   ☐ a crystal

The author compares crystals to flowers: "Crystals shine
like flowers bloom." What do you think the author meant
by this comparison?

_____

_____

From whose point of view is the poem written?
The last line of the poem is a clue.

_____

_____

Use your rhyming words from page 37 to write a poem. It can be any length. It can be about anything.

_____

_____

_____

_____

_____

_____

_____

_____

_____

A Fable

Read the **fable**. Answer the questions about each part of the story.

The Ewoks and the Duloks

Once upon a time on the forest moon of Endor, a big storm began to brew in the mountains. The Ewoks, seeing the dark clouds above the mountains, prepared for the storm. They threw ropes around the oldest trees to brace them against the wind. They dug shelters underground, which they covered with wax to make them waterproof. They gathered as many nuts and berries as they could find, and stored them away inside the shelters.

The Duloks, seeing their cousins toiling so hard, were scornful. "Why are you all working so much?" they asked.

"There is a big storm brewing in the mountains!" answered the Ewoks. "The storm is heading toward us. We are making sure we have enough to eat in case the storm lasts a long time."

• 1 •

The Duloks looked up. The sky was clear and blue, and the sun shone brightly. The passing breeze was gentle. The air smelled of almonds and lavender.

"What storm?" the Duloks answered scornfully. "It is a beautiful day! And there is plenty to eat! Why worry about storms that may come tomorrow when today is so bright and lovely?"

The Ewoks shrugged and kept right on working.

The Duloks laughed.

"What silly Ewoks you are!" they said to the Ewoks, and went off to play.

• 2 •

Where is the story set?

_____

_____

How would you describe the Ewoks?
(check as many boxes as you want)

☐ hardworking   ☐ rude   ☐ nice

☐ smart   ☐ lazy   ☐ mean

How would you describe the Duloks?
(check as many boxes as you want)

☐ hardworking   ☐ rude   ☐ nice

☐ smart   ☐ lazy   ☐ mean

How do the Ewoks know that a storm is coming?

_____

_____

Name one thing the Ewoks did to prepare for the storm.

_____

_____

What did the Duloks do while the Ewoks prepared for the storm?

_____

The next day, the storm reached the forest. The sky darkened. The wind whipped the trees. The rain poured.

In the part of the forest where the Ewoks lived, the trees that they had lashed with ropes withstood the wind. The Ewoks stayed cozy and dry deep within their shelters. Although the storm lasted several days, they had plenty of food to eat.

In the part of the forest where the Duloks lived, the trees began to fall. Their tree huts were destroyed.

The Duloks had nowhere to hide from the storm. They ran to where the Ewoks lived.

"Please, help us!" they pleaded.

The Ewoks, seeing their cousins in such distress, opened up their shelters and let them in. They shared their nuts and berries with them.

After the storm ended, the Ewoks and the Duloks left the shelters. They looked at all the damage the storm had done.

"Thank you," said the Duloks. "It was kind of you to take us in."

"When hard times hit one of us," answered the Ewoks, "they hit us all."

The End

What happened to the Duloks when the storm came?

_____

What did the Ewoks do when the Duloks went to them for help?

☐ They laughed at the Duloks.

☐ They gave them shelter.

What lesson do you think the fable teaches?

_____

_____

Spelling Break!

Write each of these spelling words two times.

people

planet

source

bright

creatures

gravity

exciting

never

laugh

shelter

course

impossible

destroy

brew

poem

white

Choose any six of the words. Write a sentence for each one.

_____

_____

_____

_____

_____

_____

_____

_____

_____

_____

An Action Story

Read the **action story**. Then answer the questions.

The Podrace

On Tatooine, podracing is a very popular sport. Fans come from all over the galaxy to watch. Podracing is also a very dangerous sport. Podracers have big engines. They fly very fast. Sometimes they crash during the race.

Anakin Skywalker is a gifted podracer. Although he is only a boy, he is one of the best racers on the planet. He has very quick reflexes. He builds his own podracers! But Anakin's mother, Shmi, does not like Anakin to race. She is afraid he will get hurt.

• 1 •

Anakin and Shmi live in a hut that is owned by Watto. They work for him. They are not allowed to work for anyone else.

One day, Qui-Gon Jinn makes a deal with Watto. If Anakin wins the podrace, Watto will let Anakin go free. So Anakin enters the race. Padmé Amidala is worried that Anakin will hurt himself, but Qui-Gon Jinn believes that Anakin is the Chosen One. He believes the Force will help Anakin win.

Finally, the race is about to begin. The stadium is full of fans. No one except for Qui-Gon Jinn, Shmi, and Padmé think that Anakin can win the podrace. Everyone knows that one of the podracers, a Dug named Sebulba, is a cheater. He will stop at nothing to win.

Ready? Set? Go! Zoom! The podracers start the race. They fly across the desert. All except for Anakin! He has trouble getting his engines to start.

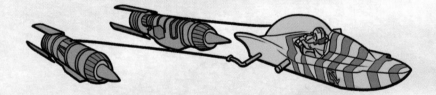

After a few minutes, Anakin starts his engines. He catches up to the other podracers by the time they get to the Canyon Dune Turn. Here they have to be careful: Tusken Raiders fire blasters at them!

• 2 •

When the podracers fly across a desert called Bindy Bend, Anakin gets hit by another podracer. For a few seconds, it looks like his engine will fall apart—but he fixes it. By the time the podracers emerge onto the Hutt Flats, the last leg of the race, Anakin is in second place. Sebulba is in first place!

The two of them fly neck and neck across the desert. Sebulba slams his podracer into Anakin's a few times, and Anakin can't turn one of his engines back on. It looks like Anakin will lose the race.

But wait—Anakin has an idea. He attaches his podracer to Sebulba's! When Sebulba tries to pull away, his podracer breaks apart. Sebulba crashes.

Anakin wins the race—and his freedom!

The End

Answer the questions about the **action story** "The Podrace."

On what planet is podracing a very popular sport?

_____

Give one reason why podracing is a dangerous sport.

_____

Who is Shmi?

_____

Name all of the characters in the story.

_____

_____

_____

Why does Qui-Gon Jinn think that Anakin will win?

_____

_____

_____

What happens to the podracers in the Canyon Dune Turn?

_____

Number the pictures from 1 to 4 to show what happened first, second, third, and fourth.

A Play

Read the **play** out loud by yourself or with friends.
Then answer the questions.

The Saga of
Anakin Skywalker

JEDI STORYTELLER: The story of Anakin Skywalker is one of the most famous stories in the galaxy. It begins a long time ago, on the desert planet Tatooine, where the boy named Anakin Skywalker lived with his mother. The Force was very strong with young Anakin.

One day, Padmé Amidala landed on Tatooine. Padmé was a few years older than Anakin. She was a Queen, but she did not wear a crown. When Anakin first saw her, he thought she was the most beautiful person he'd ever seen in his life.

ANAKIN: Are you an angel?

PADMÉ: What?

-1-

ANAKIN: An angel. I've heard the deep space pilots talk about them. They are the most beautiful creatures in the universe. They live on the Moons of Iego, I think.

PADMÉ: I've never heard of angels.

ANAKIN: You must be one . . . maybe you just don't know it.

JEDI STORYTELLER: Many years later, Padmé and Anakin met again. Anakin was no longer a little boy. He had grown up. He was a brave Jedi Padawan. A Padawan is an apprentice or a student. When Padmé's life was in danger, Anakin protected her.

Shortly afterward, they were both captured. They were taken to the Geonosian Battle Arena, where they fought fierce creatures. Padmé battled the nexu. Anakin battled the reek. They both escaped. In time, Padmé and Anakin fell in love and married.

-2-

JEDI STORYTELLER: Over time, Anakin turned to the dark side of the Force. Padmé did not like this. Nor did Obi-Wan Kenobi, Anakin's former teacher. He and Anakin had a lightsaber duel on the lava planet, Mustafar.

OBI-WAN: You have allowed this Dark Lord to twist your mind until now . . . until now you have become the very thing you swore to destroy.

ANAKIN: Don't lecture me, Obi-Wan. I see through the lies of the Jedi. I do not fear the dark side as you do. I have brought peace, justice, freedom, and security to my new Empire.

JEDI STORYTELLER: Anakin lost the lightsaber duel. Obi-Wan left him on Mustafar, but Darth Sidious rescued Anakin. Darth Sidious turned Anakin into his apprentice . . . Darth Vader.

-3-

Plot the **play** "The Saga of Anakin Skywalker."

Tell what happens in the beginning, middle, and end of the play.

Beginning

Tell about when Anakin was a little boy.

_____

_____

_____

_____

Middle

Tell about when Padmé and Anakin were taken to the Geonosian Battle Arena.

_____

_____

_____

End

Tell about when Anakin turned to the dark side of the Force.

_____

_____

_____

_____

_____

A Short Story

Read the **short story** about Boba Fett. Then answer the questions.

THE RISE OF BOBA FETT

BOBA FETT IS A LEGENDARY BOUNTY HUNTER. He can track down anybody—for a price. There is no corner of the galaxy, no space station, no remote planet in the Outer Rim, where Boba Fett won't go to find his prey.

But how did Boba Fett become a bounty hunter? It all started when he was a little boy. Boba Fett's father was the legendary Jango Fett, who had been raised by the fierce tribe of warriors known as the Mandalorians. Jango was such a supreme warrior, he was chosen to be the model for the clone trooper army. Boba was the very first clone created—an exact copy of his father. But Jango did not want Boba to be raised like the other clone troopers. Jango decided to raise him as his son. This is why Boba Fett has his own unique identity and personality.

1

Jango Fett trained Boba Fett to become a warrior. He taught him combat skills. He showed him how to use his armor, and how to fly his starfighter, the *Slave I*. When Jango died, Boba was forced to fend for himself. He relied on all the things his father had taught him to survive. Boba used his skills to become a bounty hunter.

2

A **cause** tells why something happens. An **effect** is what happens. Draw a line to match each cause and effect in the short story "The Rise of Boba Fett."

Cause

Jango Fett was a supreme warrior.

Jango raised Boba as his son.

Jango died.

Effect

Boba was forced to fend for himself.

Jango was chosen to become the model for the clone trooper army.

Boba has his own unique identity and personality.

 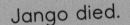

Jedi Stories!

Read the **stories** about the Jedi. Then answer the questions.

Ki-Adi-Mundi was a member of the Jedi Council. He was born on the planet Cerea. When he was four years old, he became a Padawan, an apprentice, to Master Yoda. He was a very powerful Jedi, and could move objects with his mind.

Ki-Adi-Mundi was exceptionally brave, and carried a blue-bladed lightsaber. Sadly, his clone troopers turned on him on Mygeeto, after Order 66 was activated.

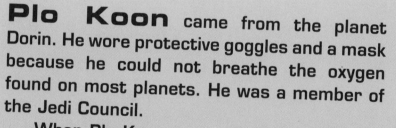

Plo Koon came from the planet Dorin. He wore protective goggles and a mask because he could not breathe the oxygen found on most planets. He was a member of the Jedi Council.

When Plo Koon was a Padawan, his Jedi Master was a Wookiee named Tyvokka. In time, Plo Koon took on his own Padawan, who was named Bultar Swan.

Plo Koon's lightsaber was blue. Although he was a very skilled pilot, he died when clone troopers fired on his starfighter in Cato Neimoidia, another victim of Order 66.

Kit Fisto was a Nautolan from the planet Glee Anselm. Nautolans could live in air or underwater. Nautolans are very good swimmers because their tendrils flare out like octopus tentacles underwater.

Kit Fisto had a green-bladed lightsaber. He was a very brave Jedi. His specialty was his ability to detect what his opponent was going to do next in battle. Unfortunately, Count Dooku proved to be too strong an opponent for Kit Fisto.

Shaak Ti was a Togrutan from the planet Shili. The hollow horns on top of her head gave her the power to "hear" things that other people could not hear. This gave her an edge in battle—especially battles involving large groups.

Shaak Ti fought bravely in the Battle of Geonosis with her blue-bladed lightsaber.

Aayla Secura was a Twi'lek from the planet Ryloth. Known for her intelligence and kindness, Aayla did not like to fight. She was more of a peacemaker, only using her blue-bladed lightsaber to defend herself. Aayla was a master of Force cloaking: the ability to become so still that other people cannot detect you.

Aayla was another victim of Order 66, when the clone troopers she was leading into battle on the planet Felucia turned against her.

Order 66 was the command given that called for the immediate execution of the Jedi. The clone troopers were programmed to follow it without question or hesitation. The only person who could issue the command was Supreme Chancellor Palpatine. This was before everyone knew that he was also the Sith Lord, Darth Sidious.

Who is who? Write the name of the character on the line next to each picture.

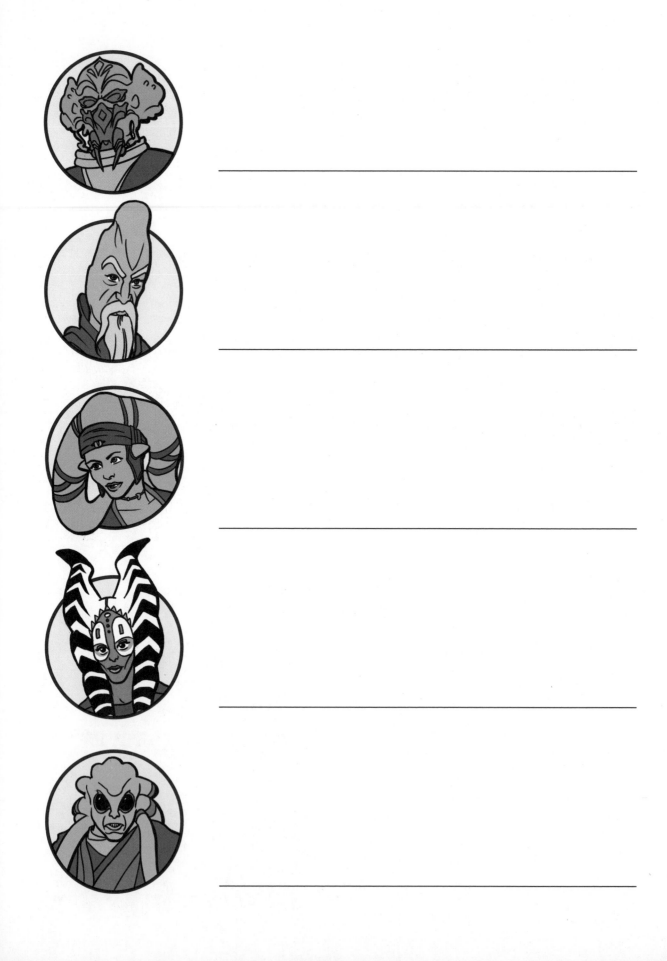

_____

_____

_____

_____

_____

There were many details in each story.
Answer the questions about the Jedi stories.

Which Jedi did not have a blue lightsaber?

_____

When Ki-Adi-Mundi was a Padawan, who was his Jedi Master?

_____

Who was responsible for issuing Order 66?

_____

_____

Which Jedi was a Twi'lek?

_____

Circle the part of Kit Fisto's body
that helps him be a good swimmer.

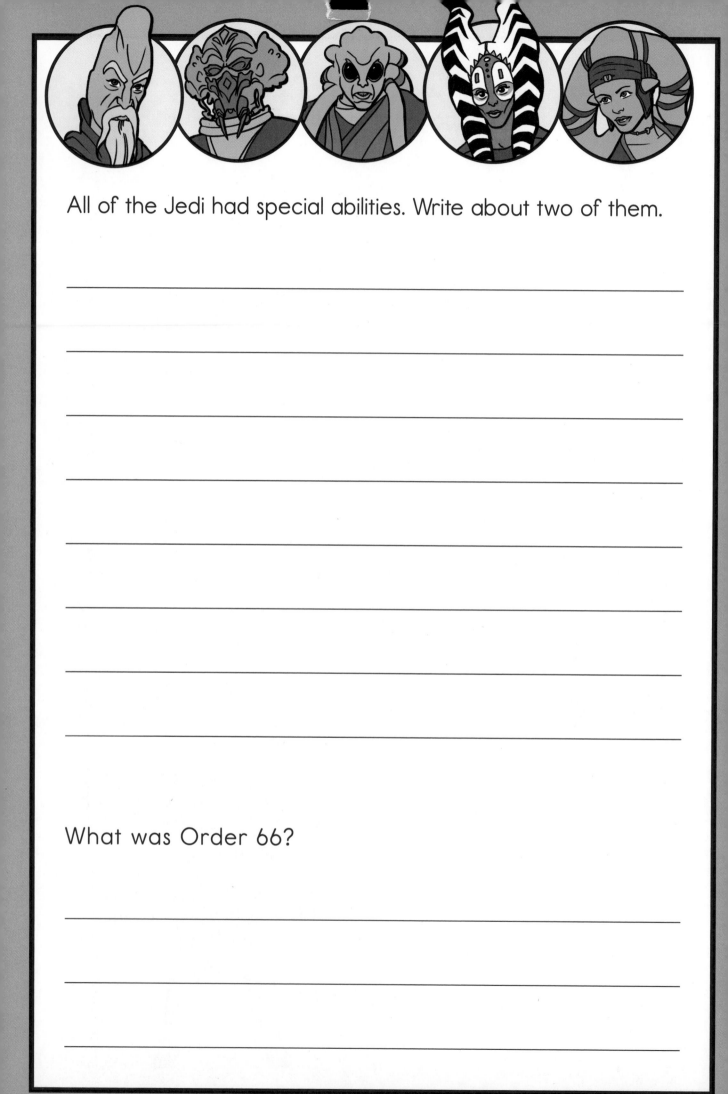

All of the Jedi had special abilities. Write about two of them.

_____

_____

_____

_____

_____

_____

_____

What was Order 66?

_____

_____

_____

A Biography

Read the **biography** of George Lucas. Then answer the questions.

George Lucas
Biography of a Filmmaker

George Walton Lucas, the creator of *Star Wars*, was born in Modesto, California, on May 14, 1944. When he was growing up, he loved comic books. Some of his early favorites were the Flash Gordon comics, which were a series of science fiction adventure stories set in outer space.

Lucas also loved cars and motor racing. He dreamed of becoming a professional race-car driver when he grew up. He started racing cars when he was a teenager. However, shortly before his high school graduation, he had a serious car accident. This accident caused him to rethink becoming a professional race-car driver.

Instead of racing cars, Lucas chose to study filmmaking at the University of Southern California. He made many student films. One of them, *THX 1138 4EB*, was a short film that received many student film awards.

1

Several years later, in 1971, Lucas founded his own movie company, Lucasfilm. The second movie Lucas made through Lucasfilm was called *American Graffiti*. The movie was inspired by Lucas's high school experiences. It was a huge hit, and was nominated for five Academy Awards.

After the release of *American Graffiti*, Lucas decided he wanted to make a space fantasy movie. He wanted it to be an adventure story set in outer space, like the Flash Gordon comics he loved so much as a kid. In the early drafts of the movie script, the story was called *The Star Wars*. By the time it came out on May 25, 1977, it was called *Star Wars*.

Star Wars quickly became the most popular movie ever made. Luke Skywalker, Princess Leia, and Darth Vader became familiar characters all over the world. People started quoting lines from the movie, such as: "May the Force be with you," or "Help me, Obi-Wan Kenobi. You're my only hope." Children wanted to play with *Star Wars* toys and games.

2

Lucas during the filming of Attack of the Clones *in Tunisia*

George Lucas had created a true pop culture phenomenon. In time, he made many other successful movies, including *The Empire Strikes Back* and *Return of the Jedi*. More than fifteen years later, he made three more *Star Wars* movies: *The Phantom Menace*, *Attack of the Clones*, and *Revenge of the Sith*. He retired from Lucasfilm in 2012, and sold his company to Disney.

It's a good thing George Lucas decided not to become a race-car driver! If he had, the world might never have had *Star Wars*!

3

Answer the questions about the biography of George Lucas.
Circle the correct answers.

What is the main idea of this biography?

a) It's the story of the creation of Lucasfilm.

b) George Lucas was born in California.

c) Don't try to become a race-car driver.

d) How George Lucas became a filmmaker and made *Star Wars*

Based on the biography, why did George Lucas decide to study filmmaking?

a) He went to the University of Southern California.

b) A race-car accident made him decide not to become a race-car driver.

c) He had always loved movies.

d) He founded Lucasfilm.

What was the name of the movie that came out in 1977?

a) *American Graffiti*

b) *Star Wars*

c) *THX 1138 4EB*

d) *Flash Gordon*

What happened when *Star Wars* came out?

a) It became the most popular movie of all time.

b) George Lucas decided to retire.

c) George Lucas created *American Graffiti*.

d) George Lucas founded Lucasfilm.

CINEMA
1 **STAR WARS**
12 230 5 730 10 PG

Circle the best word to complete each sentence.

George Lucas _____ cars and motor racing.

disliked   loved   liked

American Graffiti was _____ by George Lucas's high school experience.

made   loved   inspired

George Lucas wanted to make an _____ story set in outer space.

exciting   adventure   upsetting

After *Star Wars* came out, Darth Vader became a _____ character to people around the world.

familiar   hated   beloved

Based on the text, why is it a good thing that George Lucas did not become a race-car driver?

_____

_____

Spelling Break!

Write each of these spelling words two times.

popular _____ _____

first _____ _____

beautiful _____ _____

student _____ _____

clone _____ _____

race _____ _____

danger _____ _____

duel _____ _____

armor _____ _____

chosen _____ _____

famous _____ _____

bounty _____ _____

supreme _____ _____

vines _____ _____

driver _____ _____

Choose any six of the words. Write a sentence for each one.

_____

_____

_____

_____

_____

_____

_____

_____

_____

A Letter to George Lucas

Here is a fan letter to George Lucas. The parts of the letter have been labeled, but there are some grammatical mistakes. Use the proofreading marks below to edit the mistakes.

∧ Add text	⊙ Add a period	⇗ Add a question mark
≡ Capitalize letter	ℒ Take out	◯ Spelling error

Mr. George Lucas ← Heading

Lucasfilm

1110 Gorgas Avenue

San Francisco, CA 94129

Body

Dear Mr Lucas, ← Greeting

   I love your movies! I like all six of them, but my favorite is Attak of the Clones. it was cool how Padmé, Obi-Wan, and anakin fight the arena creatures. I also liked how the clone troopers helped the the Jedi.

   I heard you are making three new movies. Will those be about Luke Skywalker I can't wait to see them.

Sincerely, ← Closing

Cary (age 10) ← Signature

A Letter From You

Would you like to write a letter to George Lucas?

Write a first draft of it here.

_____

_____

_____

_____

_____

_____

_____

_____

Now proofread your letter to make sure you haven't made any mistakes.

Use the checklist at right to make sure!

☐ Are all the words spelled correctly?

☐ Are paragraphs indented?

☐ Does every sentence begin with a capital letter?

☐ Does every sentence end with a period or a question mark?

☐ Are names capitalized?

☐ Do you have a heading, greeting, body, closing, and signature?

An Article

Read the newspaper **article**. Then answer the questions.

May 26, 1977

In a Galaxy Far, Far Away. . . .

A review of a new movie called *Star Wars*

by K. Lypen

LOS ANGELES, CALIFORNIA–
Yesterday, *Star Wars: A New Hope* opened in movie theaters across the country. Written and directed by George Lucas, this science fiction movie is a fun and exciting adventure through outer space.

The plot revolves around Luke Skywalker, a young man living on a remote desert planet. Luke craves adventure. He wants to become a Jedi Knight, like his father had been. When a couple of droids land on his planet, he doesn't realize that his quest for adventure is about to come true.

The droids lead Luke to Obi-Wan Kenobi, a wise, old hermit living in the desert. Obi-Wan, it turns out, is a Jedi Knight himself. He starts to train Luke Skywalker in the ways of the Force.

The Force is an energy field that lives inside and around all living things. Its powers can be used for good—or evil.

Together with the two droids, a smart-mouthed pilot named Han Solo, and a furry creature named Chewbacca, Luke and Obi-Wan set out to rescue Princess Leia. Leia is part of the Rebel Alliance that is working to defeat the evil Empire. She's been taken prisoner by Darth Vader. Vader was once a pupil of Obi-Wan Kenobi, who had trained him to become a Jedi Knight. That was before Vader turned to the dark side of the Force. Now Vader uses his Force powers for evil on behalf of the Empire.

Will the Rebel Alliance defeat the Empire? Will Luke become a Jedi Knight? This movie is destined to become a classic. It is a thrilling adventure story that everyone in the family will love. Two thumbs up!

The sentences below are all highlighted in the article.

Put a check mark by the meaning that fits the underlined word in each sentence.

Luke craves adventure.

☐ wants   ☐ hates

The droids lead Luke to Obi-Wan Kenobi, a wise, old hermit living in the desert.

☐ thoughtful   ☐ friend

Vader was once a pupil of Obi-Wan Kenobi, who had trained him to become a Jedi Knight.

☐ teacher   ☐ student

Now Vader uses his Force powers for evil on behalf of the Empire.

☐ on half of   ☐ on the side of

Will the Rebel Alliance defeat the Empire?

☐ beat   ☐ lose to

Draw a line from the vocabulary words used in the article (in the blue boxes) to the words that mean the same thing (in the yellow boxes).

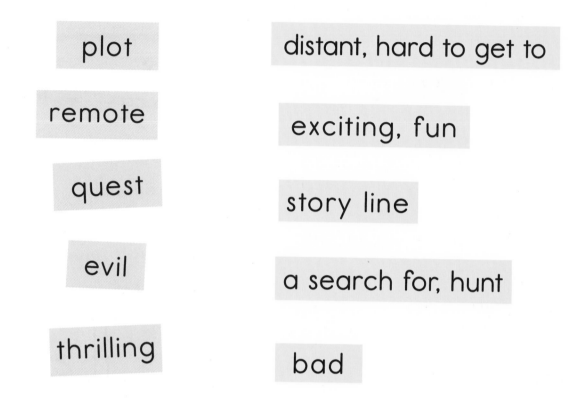

plot

remote

quest

evil

thrilling

distant, hard to get to

exciting, fun

story line

a search for, hunt

bad

Write a sentence for each of the words.

_____

_____

_____

_____

All About Lightsabers!

Read the **essay** about lightsabers. Then answer the questions.

LIGHTSABERS

The favorite weapons of both the Jedi and the Sith, lightsabers are extremely powerful—but only in the hands of those who know how to use them! With blades made of pure energy, they can cut through anything (except another lightsaber).

Most Jedi have blue- or green-bladed lightsabers.* Jedi construct their own lightsabers from crystals they collect on Ilum, a mountainous ice planet. The lightsaber hilt is a complicated piece of machinery (see chart at right). Every Jedi designs his or her own lightsaber to suit his or her needs.

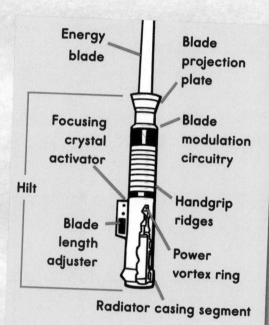

Energy blade
Blade projection plate
Focusing crystal activator
Blade modulation circuitry
Hilt
Handgrip ridges
Blade length adjuster
Power vortex ring
Radiator casing segment

The Sith also make their own lightsabers. They are always red because they use the dark side of the Force.

* Footnote: Mace Windu's lightsaber is an exception to this. His lightsaber is purple because of his unique connection with the Force.

Answer the questions about the essay on lightsabers.

What is the main idea of this essay?

_____

_____

_____

_____

What color lightsabers do the Sith have? Why?

_____

_____

What is the only thing that lightsabers cannot cut through?

_____

What is the footnote about?

_____

Look at the chart. What is the black button on the lightsaber called?

_____

An Origami Lightsaber

Follow the **instructions** to fold four origami lightsabers.

Use the artwork on page 81 as the origami paper.

HOW TO FOLD A LIGHTSABER

1 | Cut along the dotted lines on page 81. Place the paper for one lightsaber with the arrow pointing up.

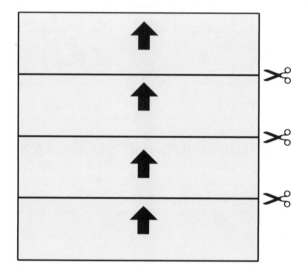

2 Fold just enough to form a thin flap on the left side.

3 Fold and unfold in half, lengthwise. Then unfold.

4 Fold the top and the bottom lengthwise to the middle crease. Then unfold.

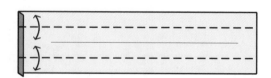

5 Fold in the bottom right corner. Then unfold. Turn the page over.

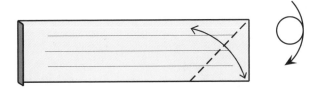

6 Fold in the right side.

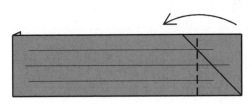

7 Fold the corners (marked A) into the pockets (marked B). This will turn the model into a triangular tube.

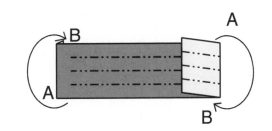

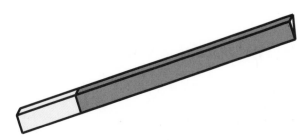

Answer the questions about the origami lightsaber **instructions**.

In Step 3, the instructions tell you to fold and unfold in half "lengthwise." What does "lengthwise" mean?

a) along the long part of the paper

b) diagonally

c) left to right

What step in the instructions tells when to turn the paper over?

_____

After following the instructions for step 7, the model

will turn into a _____ tube.

How many lightsabers were you able to fold?

_____

Start with this
side facing you.

Start with this
side facing you.

Start with this
side facing you.

Start with this
side facing you.

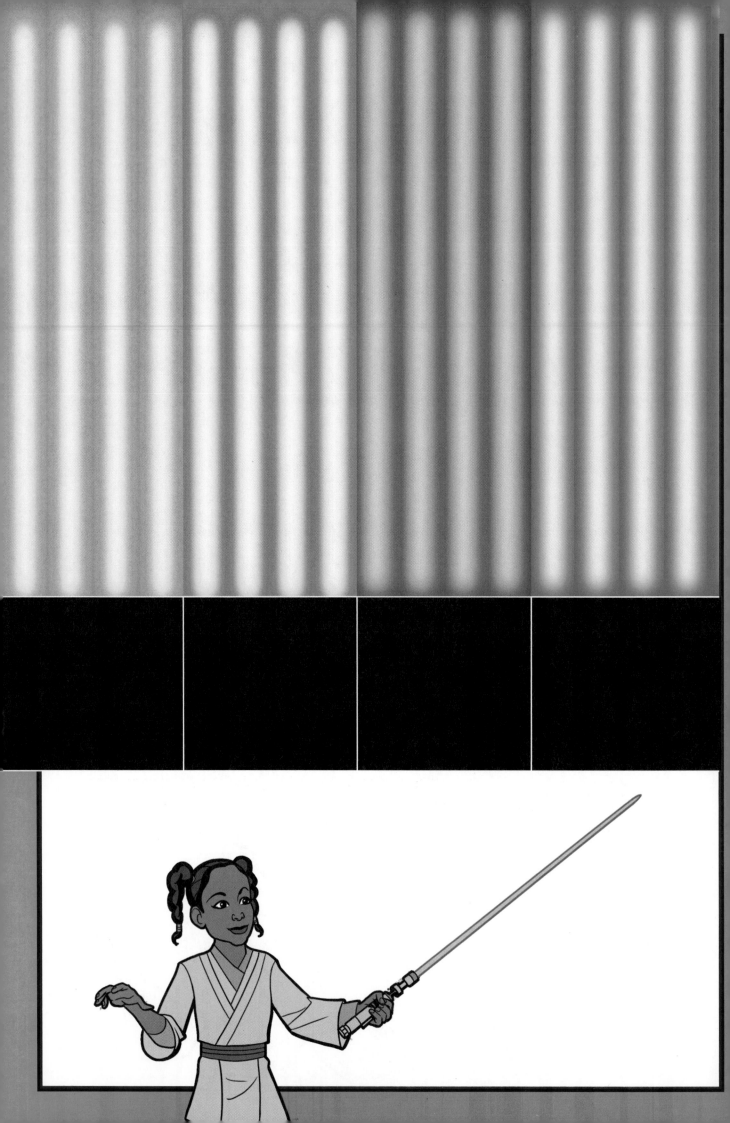

Time to Alphabetize

Write all the words in the column on the left in **alphabetical order** on the right.

hermit

sincerely

train

footnote

purple

essay

diagonal

attack

character

detests

quest

_____

_____

_____

_____

_____

_____

_____

_____

_____

_____

_____

Choose any two words and use them in a sentence.

_____

_____

Galactic History!

The history of the *Star Wars* saga is quite complicated. A **timeline** is a good tool to use to organize events. It can show us how much time has passed between different events and help readers visualize how events all fit together.

41 BBY

Anakin Skywalker, the Chosen One, who will bring balance to the Force, is born.

34 BBY

Anakin Skywalker begins to build C-3PO.

32 BBY

Padmé Amidala, former Princess of Theed, is elected Queen of Naboo.

The Trade Federation begins the blockade of Naboo.

Qui-Gon Jinn meets Anakin Skywalker on the planet Tatooine.

The creation of a secret clone army begins on Kamino. Jango Fett, a bounty hunter who wears Mandalorian armor, is the model for the clones.

22 BBY

Shmi Skywalker, Anakin's mother, is captured by the Tusken Raiders.

The Clone Wars begin with the Battle of Geonosis.

Anakin Skywalker and Padmé Amidala marry in secret on Naboo.

19 BBY

Chancellor Palpatine is revealed to be the Sith Master Darth Sidious.

Anakin Skywalker turns to the dark side of the Force and becomes Darth Vader.

Order 66 is executed: Almost all the Jedi are killed.

Luke Skywalker and Leia Organa are born to Padmé Amidala, who dies after they are born.

BBY 41 40 39 38 37 36 35 34 33 32 31 30 29 28 27 26 25 24 23 22 21 20 19

BBY stands for Before the Battle of Yavin

Read the **timeline**.

Then answer the questions.

4 ABY

Han Solo is rescued from Jabba the Hutt.

Yoda dies.

The shield generator is destroyed with the help of the Ewoks in the Battle of Endor.

Darth Vader turns on Palpatine to save Luke's life.

Darth Vader dies after turning back to the light side of the Force.

Without the protection of the shield generator, the Death Star is destroyed by Lando Calrissian, Wedge Antilles, and Nien Nunb.

The fall of the Empire and the death of Palpatine are celebrated throughout the galaxy.

0 BBY

Princess Leia is captured by Darth Vader.

C-3PO and R2-D2 land on Tatooine where they are found by Luke Skywalker. Luke helps them on their mission to find Obi-Wan Kenobi.

Alderaan is destroyed by the Death Star.

Darth Vader strikes down Obi-Wan Kenobi, allowing Obi-Wan to become one with the Force.

Luke Skywalker destroys the Death Star in the Battle of Yavin.

3 ABY

The Battle of Hoth takes place when the Empire discovers the Alliance's secret base on the ice planet.

Luke Skywalker begins his Jedi training with Yoda on the planet Dagobah.

Boba Fett captures Han Solo, who is frozen in carbonite on Cloud City.

Lando Calrissian joins the Rebel Alliance.

Darth Vader reveals to Luke that he is his father.

15 14 13 12 11 10 9 8 7 6 5 4 3 2 1 0 1 2 3 4 ABY

ABY stands for After the Battle of Yavin

Answer the questions about the galactic **timeline**.

The timeline begins with what major event?

_____

In 4 ABY, whose life did Darth Vader save?

_____

In what year did the Battle of Hoth take place? _____

In what year was Princess Leia caught by Darth Vader?

_____

Name two events that happened in 22 BBY.

_____

_____

In your opinion, what was the most exciting event that happened before the Battle of Yavin? Why?

_____

_____

What was the most exciting event that happened after the Battle of Yavin?

_____

_____

Draw a picture of your favorite scene from the timeline.

Start Your Timeline!

On this page, make a list of the most important events in your life, starting with the year you were born. Include things like when you first started to talk and when you started school. List nine events.

_____

_____

_____

_____

_____

_____

_____

Make Your Own Timeline!

Using the list of important life events you made on page 88, create your own **timeline**.

Write the date, or just the year, and an important event in each box. Then draw a line from each box to the timeline at the bottom.

Date _____

Event <u>I was born on</u> _____

_____

_____

_____

Date _____

Event _____

_____

_____

_____

Date _____

Event _____

_____

_____

_____

_____

Date _____

Event _____

_____

_____

_____

_____

Date of birth	1 year old	2 years old	3 years old	4 years old	5 years old

Date _____

Event _____

_____

_____

Date _____

Event _____

_____

_____

Date _____

Event _____

_____

_____

Date _____

Event _____

_____

_____

_____

Date _____

Event _____

_____

_____

_____

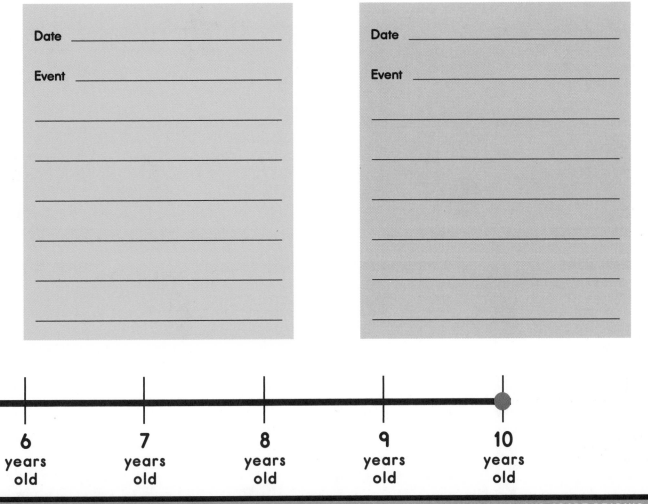

6
years
old

7
years
old

8
years
old

9
years
old

10
years
old

Answers

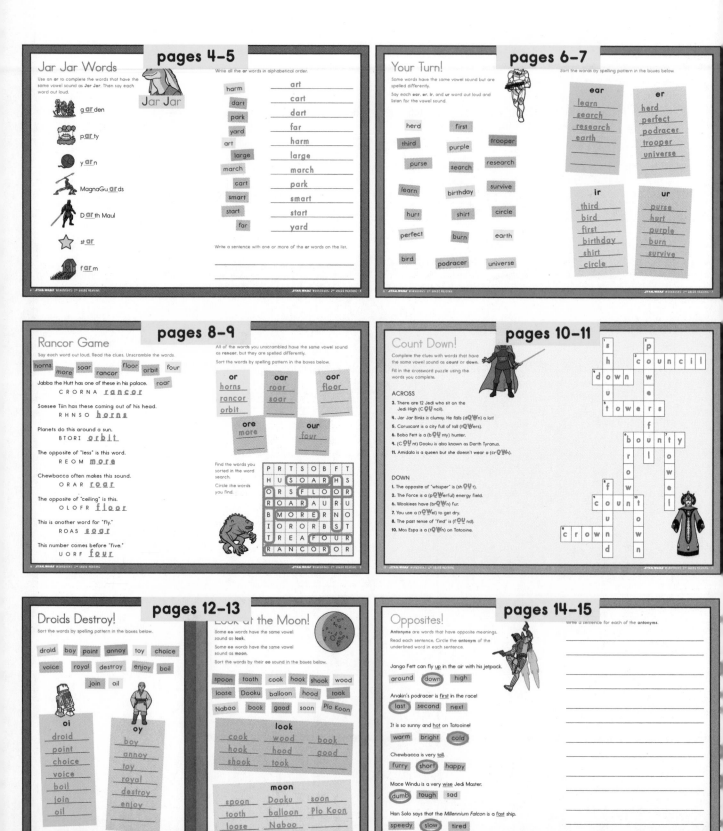

pages 4–5

Jar Jar Words

Use an **ar** to complete the words that have the same vowel sound as Jar Jar. Then say each word out loud.

Jar Jar

g **ar** den

p **ar** ty

y **ar** n

MagnaGu **ar** ds

D **ar** th Maul

st **ar**

f **ar** m

Write all the **ar** words in alphabetical order.

harm	art
dart	cart
park	dart
yard	far
art	harm
large	large
march	march
cart	park
smart	smart
start	start
far	yard

Write a sentence with one or more of the **ar** words on the list.

pages 6–7

Your Turn!

Some words have the same vowel sound but are spelled differently.

Say each **ear**, **er**, **ir**, and **ur** word out loud and listen for the vowel sound.

herd, first, third, purple, trooper, purse, search, research, learn, birthday, survive, hurt, shirt, circle, perfect, burn, earth, bird, podracer, universe

ear
learn
search
research
earth

er
herd
perfect
podracer
trooper
universe

ir
third
bird
first
birthday
shirt
circle

ur
purse
hurt
purple
burn
survive

pages 8–9

Rancor Game

Say each word out loud. Read the clues. Unscramble the words.

horns, more, soar, rancor, floor, orbit, four, roar

Jabba the Hutt has one of these in his palace.
C R O R N A **rancor**

Saesee Tiin has these coming out of his head.
R H N S O **horns**

Planets do this around a sun.
B T O R I **orbit**

The opposite of "less" is this word.
R E O M **more**

Chewbacca often makes this sound.
O R A R **roar**

The opposite of "ceiling" is this.
O L O F R **floor**

This is another word for "fly."
R O A S **soar**

This number comes before "five."
U O R F **four**

All of the words you unscrambled have the same vowel sound as **rancor**, but they are spelled differently.

Sort the words by spelling pattern in the boxes below.

or
horns
rancor
orbit

oar
roar
soar

oor
floor

ore
more

our
four

Find the words you sorted in the word search.

Circle the words you find.

P	R	T	S	O	B	F	T
H	U	S	O	A	R	H	S
O	R	S	F	L	O	O	R
R	O	A	R	A	U	R	U
B	M	O	R	E	R	N	O
I	O	R	O	R	B	S	T
T	R	E	A	F	O	U	R
R	A	N	C	O	R	O	R

pages 10–11

Count Down!

Complete the clues with words that have the same vowel sound as **count** or **down**.

Fill in the crossword puzzle using the words you complete.

ACROSS

3. There are 12 Jedi who sit on the Jedi High (C**OU**ncil).
4. Jar Jar Binks is clumsy. He falls (d**OW**n) a lot!
5. Coruscant is a city full of tall (t**OW**ers).
6. Boba Fett is a (b**OU**nty) hunter.
9. (C**OU**nt) Dooku is also known as Darth Tyranus.
11. Amidala is a queen but she doesn't wear a (cr**OW**n).

DOWN

1. The opposite of "whisper" is (sh**OU**t).
2. The Force is a (p**OW**erful) energy field.
6. Wookiees have (br**OW**n) fur.
7. You use a (t**OW**el) to get dry.
8. The past tense of "find" is (f**OU**nd).
10. Mos Espa is a (t**OW**n) on Tatooine.

Crossword grid:
council, down, towers, bounty, count, crown, shout, powerful, brown, towel, found, town

pages 12–13

Droids Destroy!

Sort the words by spelling pattern in the boxes below.

droid, boy, point, annoy, toy, choice, voice, royal, destroy, enjoy, boil, join, oil

oi
droid
point
choice
voice
boil
join
oil

oy
boy
annoy
toy
royal
destroy
enjoy

Look at the Moon!

Some **oo** words have the same vowel sound as **look**.

Some **oo** words have the same vowel sound as **moon**.

Sort the words by their **oo** sound in the boxes below.

spoon, tooth, cook, hook, shook, wood, loose, Dooku, balloon, hood, took, Naboo, book, good, soon, Plo Koon

look
cook, wood, book
hook, hood, good
shook, took

moon
spoon, Dooku, soon
tooth, balloon, Plo Koon
loose, Naboo

pages 14–15

Opposites!

Antonyms are words that have opposite meanings. Read each sentence. Circle the **antonym** of the underlined word in each sentence.

Jango Fett can fly <u>up</u> in the air with his jetpack.
around **down** high

Anakin's podracer is <u>first</u> in the race!
last second next

It is so sunny and <u>hot</u> on Tatooine!
warm bright **cold**

Chewbacca is very <u>tall</u>.
furry **short** happy

Mace Windu is a very <u>wise</u> Jedi Master.
dumb tough sad

Han Solo says that the Millennium Falcon is a <u>fast</u> ship.
speedy **slow** tired

Write a sentence for each of the **antonyms**.

Similars!

Synonyms are words that have similar meanings.
Read each sentence. Circle the **synonym** of the underlined word in each sentence.

Write a sentence for each of the synonyms.

_____
_____
_____
_____

Yoda may be the smallest Jedi, but he is also the most underlined powerful.

happy   weak   (strong)

C-3PO can speak over six million languages.

silent   (talk)   sing

R2-D2 is tiny compared to C-3PO.

big   same   (little)

Padmé is brave when she battles the nexu.

(fearless)   scared   sleepy

Many Imperial officers are scared of Darth Vader.

unafraid   (frightened)   loyal

Chewbacca is Han Solo's best friend.

enemy   only   (greatest)

Night, Knight!

Homophones are words that sound the same but have different spellings and meanings.
Read each sentence. Circle the correct **homophone**.

Write a sentence for each homophone that you did not circle.

_____
_____
_____
_____
_____
_____
_____

Luke is a Jedi (Knight) / Night.

The some / (sum) of three plus three is six.

Tatooine has two (suns) / sons.

Princess Leia is on a (peace) / piece mission.

No one (guessed) / guest that Luke was Leia's brother!

Rancors eat a lot of meet / (meat).

Beru is Luke's ant / (aunt).

Batches of Lightsabers!

Plural means more than one. For most words, add **s** to make a singular noun plural. For words ending in **sh, ch, tch, s,** or **x,** add **es.**
Write the plural for each word by adding **s** or **es.**

lightsaber **s**   batch **es**

tree **s**   box **es**

glass **es**   bench **es**

bush **es**   bus **es**

Ewok **s**   watch **es**

stormtrooper **s**   ax **es**

Weird Plurals!

Some singular nouns do not take a **s** or **es** to form plurals. These nouns have **irregular plurals.** An irregular plural changes the spelling of the word.
Draw a line from the noun to its **irregular plural.**

tooth — teeth
child — children
goose — geese
foot — feet
woman — women
man — men
mouse — mice
person — people
ox — oxen

Write each of the irregular plurals on the lines below.

mice   feet   children
teeth   geese   women
men   people oxen

Tell Me Something!

A **sentence** is a group of words that expresses a complete thought.
Read each group of words. Underline the complete **sentences.**

Remember, you always begin a sentence with a capital letter and end with a period.

<u>Tusken Raiders live in tents.</u>

The stars in the galaxy.

Luke, Leia, and Han.

<u>Chewbacca can fly the *Millennium Falcon.*</u>

The small, furry Ewok.

<u>C-3PO is very shiny.</u>

<u>Darth Vader wears a mask.</u>

The droids you're looking for.

<u>It happened a long time ago.</u>

Write a complete sentence for each group of words that you did not underline.

_____
_____
_____
_____
_____
_____
_____

Question or Statement?

A **question** is a sentence that asks something.
A **statement** is a sentence that tells what someone or something is doing, or what someone or something is.
Copy each sentence on the line below it.
Add a question mark if the sentence asks a **question.**
Add a period if the sentence is a **statement.**

How many Ewoks do you see
How many Ewoks do you see?

Will Anakin become a Jedi Knight
Will Anakin become a Jedi Knight?

He wears a black robe
He wears a black robe.

Who is looking for Obi-Wan Kenobi
Who is looking for Obi-Wan Kenobi?

Will Lando help Han escape
Will Lando help Han escape?

Padmé loves Anakin
Padmé loves Anakin.

Exclamations and Commands!

An **exclamation** is a sentence that shows a strong feeling.
A **command** is a sentence that tells someone to do something.
Copy each **sentence** on the line below it.
Add an exclamation point to turn each into an **exclamation** or a **command.**

We need to get out of this asteroid field
We need to get out of this asteroid field!

Watch out.
Watch out!

I thought you said this ship was fast.
I thought you said this ship was fast!

Go faster.
Go faster!

That asteroid is coming right at us.
That asteroid is coming right at us!

We did it.
We did it!

Common or Proper?

A **common noun** is a word that refers to a person, place, or thing.
A **proper noun** is a word or group of words that names a specific person, place, or thing.
Underline the **common nouns** in each sentence.
Draw a circle around the **proper nouns.**

(Anakin) uses many different <u>tools</u> to build the <u>droid.</u>

(Queen Amidala) comes from (Naboo.)

Both the <u>Jedi</u> and the (Sith) use <u>lightsabers.</u>

The <u>moons</u> orbit around the <u>planets</u> because of <u>gravity.</u>

Many strange <u>creatures</u> live in the <u>swamps</u> of (Dagobah.)

Sort all the **nouns** you underlined and circled in the boxes below. Don't forget to capitalize the proper nouns.

person	place	thing
Anakin	Naboo	tools
Queen	moons	droid
Amidala	planets	lightsabers
Jedi	swamps	gravity
Sith	Dagobah	creatures

Pronouns!

A **pronoun** is a word that can take the place of a noun. Read the **pronouns** in the boxes.
Rewrite each sentence with a **pronoun** in place of the underlined word or words.

He   She   It   We   They

Kit Fisto and Plo Koon fight the droids.
They fight the droids.

Aayla joins the battle.
She joins the battle.

Mace Windu comes to help.
He comes to help.

Mace says, "All of us are stronger than they are!"
Mace says, "We are stranger than they are!"

He quickly destroys a droid with his lightsaber.
He quickly destroys it with his lightsaber.

Younglings!

The **subject** tells who or what a sentence is about.
The subject can have a **noun** or **pronoun.**

Underline the **subject.** Circle the **noun** in the subject.

The Jedi (Temple) is an exciting place.

(Younglings) from every part of the galaxy become Jedi Knights.

(Yoda) teaches the younglings every day.

The tallest (youngling) is called Gungi.

(Gungi) is a Wookiee.

All the (younglings) train and play together.

If (they) train hard, they may grow up to be Jedi Masters like Yoda!

An **adjective** describes a noun.
Color, size, and number words are **adjectives.**
Circle the **noun.** Underline the **adjective** or **adjectives.**

furry (Wookiee)
blue (lightsaber)
green (skin)
five brave (younglings)
big (rock)
two (eyes)

Jedi Knights!

A **verb** is an action word. It tells what someone or something does.
A **present-tense verb** tells what is happening now.
Use the **action words** below to tell what the Jedi Knights are doing.

fixes   talks   jumps
walks   picks   climbs

Kit Fisto **walks** a bantha down the road.

Aayla Secura **picks** a flower.

Plo Koon **talks** to Bultar Swan about the weather.

Saesee Tiin **fixes** the droid with his tools.

Luminara Unduli **jumps** over the puddle.

Shaak Ti **climbs** up a tower.

A **past-tense verb** tells what happened in the past. You add **ed** to make many verbs **past tense.**
Rewrite each sentence on the previous page in the past tense by changing the **s** or **es** with **ed.**

Kit Fisto walked a bantha down the road.

Aayla Secura picked a flower.

Plo Koon talked to Bultar Swan about the weather.

Saesee Tiin fixed the droid with his tools.

Luminara Unduli jumped over the puddle.

Shaak Ti climbed up a tower.

Answers

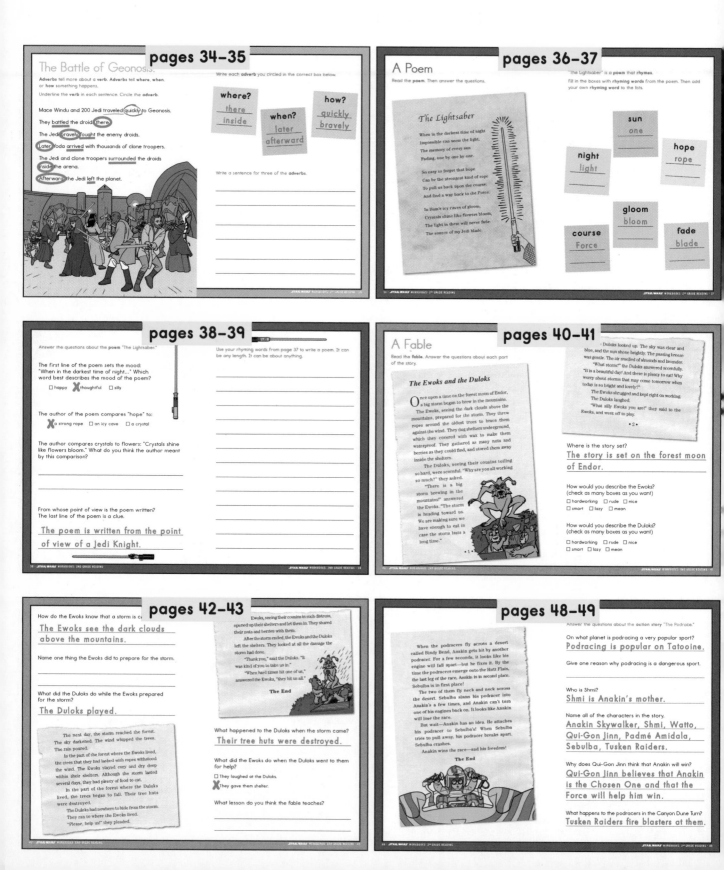

pages 34–35

The Battle of Geonosis

Adverbs tell more about a **verb**. **Adverbs** tell **where**, **when**, or **how** something happens.

Underline the **verb** in each sentence. Circle the **adverb**.

Mace Windu and 200 Jedi traveled (quickly) to Geonosis.

They battled the droid (there).

The Jedi (bravely) fought the enemy droids.

(Later) Yoda arrived with thousands of clone troopers.

The Jedi and clone troopers surrounded the droids (inside) the arena.

(Afterward) the Jedi left the planet.

Write each **adverb** you circled in the correct box below.

where? there inside

when? later afterward

how? quickly bravely

Write a sentence for three of the **adverbs**.

pages 36–37

A Poem

Read the **poem**. Then answer the questions.

"The Lightsaber" is a **poem** that **rhymes**.

Fill in the boxes with **rhyming** words from the poem. Then add your own **rhyming** word to the lists.

The Lightsaber

When in the darkest time of night
Impossible can seem the light.
The memory of every sun
Fading, one by one by one.

So easy to forget that hope
Can be the strongest kind of rope
To pull us back upon the course:
And find a way back to the Force.

In Ilum's icy caves of gloom,
Crystals shine like flowers bloom,
The light in them will never fade.
The source of my Jedi blade.

sun one

night light

hope rope

gloom bloom

course Force

fade blade

pages 38–39

Answer the questions about the **poem** "The Lightsaber."

The first line of the poem sets the mood: "When in the darkest time of night..." Which word best describes the mood of the poem?

☐ happy ☒ thoughtful ☐ silly

The author of the poem compares "hope" to:

☒ a strong rope ☐ an icy cave ☐ a crystal

The author compares crystals to flowers: "Crystals shine like flowers bloom." What do you think the author meant by this comparison?

From whose point of view is the poem written? The last line of the poem is a clue.

The poem is written from the point of view of a Jedi Knight.

Use your rhyming words from page 37 to write a poem. It can be any length. It can be about anything.

pages 40–41

A Fable

Read the **fable**. Answer the questions about each part of the story.

The Ewoks and the Duloks

Once upon a time on the forest moon of Endor, a big storm began to brew in the mountains.

The Ewoks, seeing the dark clouds above the mountains, prepared for the storm. They threw ropes around the oldest trees to brace them against the wind. They dug shelters underground, which they covered with wax to make them waterproof. They gathered as many nuts and berries as they could find, and stored them away inside the shelters.

The Duloks, seeing their cousins toiling so hard, were scornful. "Why are you all working so much?" they asked.

"There is a big storm brewing in the mountains!" answered the Ewoks. "The storm is heading toward us. We are making sure we have enough to eat in case the storm lasts a long time."

The Duloks looked up. The sky was clear and blue, and the sun shone brightly. The passing breeze was gentle. The air smelled of almonds and lavender.

"What storm?" the Duloks answered scornfully. "It is a beautiful day! And there is plenty to eat! Why worry about storms that may come tomorrow when today is so so bright and lovely?"

The Ewoks shrugged and kept right on working. The Duloks laughed.

"What silly Ewoks you are!" they said to the Ewoks, and went off to play.

• 2 •

Where is the story set?

The story is set on the forest moon of Endor.

How would you describe the Ewoks? (check as many boxes as you want)

☐ hardworking ☐ rude ☐ nice
☐ smart ☐ lazy ☐ mean

How would you describe the Duloks? (check as many boxes as you want)

☐ hardworking ☐ rude ☐ nice
☐ smart ☐ lazy ☐ mean

pages 42–43

How do the Ewoks know that a storm is c...

The Ewoks see the dark clouds above the mountains.

Name one thing the Ewoks did to prepare for the storm.

What did the Duloks do while the Ewoks prepared for the storm?

The Duloks played.

The next day, the storm reached the forest. The sky darkened. The wind whipped the trees. The rain poured.

In the part of the forest where the Ewoks lived, the trees that they had lashed with ropes withstood the wind. The Ewoks stayed cozy and dry deep within their shelters. Although the storm lasted several days, they had plenty of food to eat.

In the part of the forest where the Duloks lived, the trees began to fall. Their tree huts were destroyed.

The Duloks had nowhere to hide from the storm. They ran to where the Ewoks lived. "Please, help us!" they pleaded.

The Ewoks, seeing their cousins in such distress, opened up their shelters and let them in. They shared their nuts and berries with them.

After the storm ended, the Ewoks and the Duloks left the shelters. They looked at all the damage the storm had done.

"Thank you," said the Duloks. "It was kind of you to take us in."

"When hard times hit one of us," answered the Ewoks, "they hit us all."

The End

What happened to the Duloks when the storm came?

Their tree huts were destroyed.

What did the Ewoks do when the Duloks went to them for help?

☐ They laughed at the Duloks.
☒ They gave them shelter.

What lesson do you think the fable teaches?

pages 48–49

Answer the questions about the action story "The Podrace."

When the podracers fly across a desert called Bindy Bend, Anakin gets hit by another podracer. For a few seconds, it looks like his engine will fall apart—but he fixes it. By the time the podracers emerge onto the Hutt Flats, the last leg of the race, Anakin is in second place. Sebulba is in first place!

The two of them fly neck and neck across the desert. Sebulba slams his podracer into Anakin's a few times, and Anakin can't turn one of his engines back on. It looks like Anakin will lose the race.

But wait—Anakin has an idea. He attaches his podracer to Sebulba's! When Sebulba tries to pull away, his podracer breaks apart. Sebulba crashes.

Anakin wins the race—and his freedom!

The End

On what planet is podracing a very popular sport?

Podracing is popular on Tatooine.

Give one reason why podracing is a dangerous sport.

Who is Shmi?

Shmi is Anakin's mother.

Name all of the characters in the story.

Anakin Skywalker, Shmi, Watto, Qui-Gon Jinn, Padmé Amidala, Sebulba, Tusken Raiders.

Why does Qui-Gon Jinn think that Anakin will win?

Qui-Gon Jinn believes that Anakin is the Chosen One and that the Force will help him win.

What happens to the podracers in the Canyon Dune Turn?

Tusken Raiders fire blasters at them.

Number the pictures from 1 to 4 to show what happened first, second, third, and fourth.

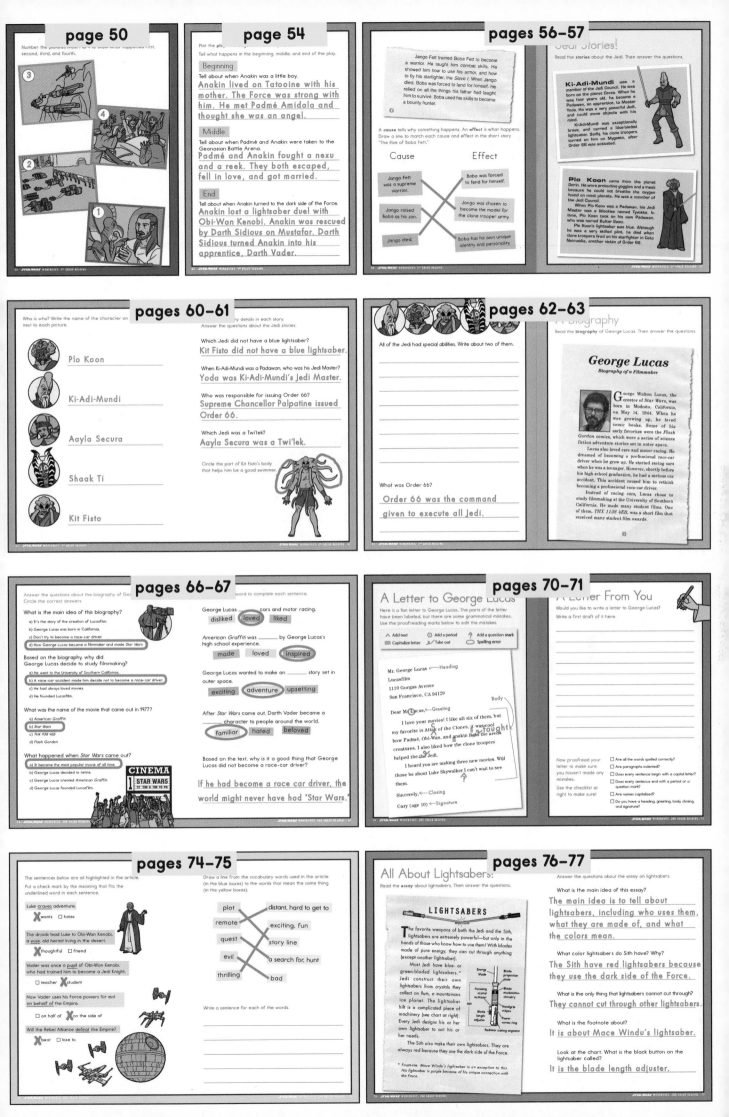

Plot the plot.
Tell what happens in the beginning, middle, and end of the play.

Beginning
Tell about when Anakin was a little boy.
Anakin lived on Tatooine with his mother. The Force was strong with him. He met Padmé Amidala and thought she was an angel.

Middle
Tell about when Padmé and Anakin were taken to the Geonosian Battle Arena.
Padmé and Anakin fought a nexu and a reek. They both escaped, fell in love, and got married.

End
Tell about when Anakin turned to the dark side of the Force.
Anakin lost a lightsaber duel with Obi-Wan Kenobi. Anakin was rescued by Darth Sidious on Mustafar. Darth Sidious turned Anakin into his apprentice, Darth Vader.

Jedi Stories!
Read the stories about the Jedi. Then answer the questions.

Jango Fett trained Boba Fett to become a warrior. He taught him combat skills. He showed him how to use his armor, and how to fly his starfighter, the *Slave I*. When Jango died, Boba was forced to fend for himself. He relied on all the things his father had taught him to survive. Boba used his skills to become a bounty hunter.

Ki-Adi-Mundi was a member of the Jedi Council. He was born on the planet Cerea. When he was four years old, he became a Padawan, an apprentice, to Master Yoda. He was a very powerful Jedi, and could move objects with his mind.
Ki-Adi-Mundi was exceptionally brave, and carried a blue-bladed lightsaber. Sadly, his clone troopers turned on him on Mygeeto, after Order 66 was activated.

A **cause** tells why something happens. An **effect** is what happens. Draw a line to match each cause and effect in the short story "The Rise of Boba Fett."

Cause

Jango Fett was a supreme warrior.

Jango raised Boba as his son.

Jango died.

Effect

Boba was forced to fend for himself.

Jango was chosen to become the model for the clone trooper army.

Boba has his own unique identity and personality.

Plo Koon came from the planet Dorin. He wore protective goggles and a mask because he could not breathe the oxygen found on most planets. He was a member of the Jedi Council.
When Plo Koon was a Padawan, his Jedi Master was a Wookiee named Tyvokka. In time, Plo Koon took on his own Padawan, who was named Bultar Swan.
Plo Koon's lightsaber was blue. Although he was a very skilled pilot, he died when clone troopers fired on his starfighter in Cato Neimoidia, another victim of Order 66.

Who is who? Write the name of the character on next to each picture.

Plo Koon

Ki-Adi-Mundi

Aayla Secura

Shaak Ti

Kit Fisto

... many details in each story.
Answer the questions about the Jedi stories.

Which Jedi did not have a blue lightsaber?
Kit Fisto did not have a blue lightsaber.

When Ki-Adi-Mundi was a Padawan, who was his Jedi Master?
Yoda was Ki-Adi-Mundi's Jedi Master.

Who was responsible for issuing Order 66?
Supreme Chancellor Palpatine issued Order 66.

Which Jedi was a Twi'lek?
Aayla Secura was a Twi'lek.

Circle the part of Kit Fisto's body that helps him be a good swimmer.

A Biography
Read the **biography** of George Lucas. Then answer the questions.

All of the Jedi had special abilities. Write about two of them.

_____
_____
_____
_____
_____

What was Order 66?
Order 66 was the command given to execute all Jedi.

George Lucas
Biography of a Filmmaker

George Walton Lucas, the creator of *Star Wars*, was born in Modesto, California, on May 14, 1944. When he was growing up, he loved comic books. Some of his early favorites were the *Flash Gordon* comics, which were a series of science fiction adventure stories set in outer space.
Lucas also loved cars and motor racing. He dreamed of becoming a professional race-car driver when he grew up. He started racing cars when he was a teenager. However, shortly before his high school graduation, he had a serious car accident. This accident caused him to rethink becoming a professional race-car driver.
Instead of racing cars, Lucas chose to study filmmaking at the University of Southern California. He made many student films. One of them, *THX 1138 4EB*, was a short film that received many student film awards.

Answer the questions about the biography of George Lucas. Circle the correct answers.

What is the main idea of this biography?
a) It's the story of the creation of Lucasfilm.
b) George Lucas was born in California.
c) Don't try to become a race-car driver.
d) How George Lucas became a filmmaker and made *Star Wars* ✓

Based on the biography, why did George Lucas decide to study filmmaking?
a) He went to the University of Southern California.
b) A race-car accident made him decide not to become a race-car driver. ✓
c) He had always loved movies.
d) He founded Lucasfilm.

What was the name of the movie that came out in 1977?
a) *American Graffiti*
b) *Star Wars* ✓
c) *THX 1138 4EB*
d) *Flash Gordon*

What happened when *Star Wars* came out?
a) It became the most popular movie of all time. ✓
b) George Lucas decided to retire.
c) George Lucas created *American Graffiti*.
d) George Lucas founded Lucasfilm.

... word to complete each sentence.

George Lucas _____ cars and motor racing.
disliked **loved** liked

American Graffiti was _____ by George Lucas's high school experience.
made loved **inspired**

George Lucas wanted to make an _____ story set in outer space.
exciting **adventure** upsetting

After *Star Wars* came out, Darth Vader became a _____ character to people around the world.
familiar hated beloved

Based on the text, why is it a good thing that George Lucas did not become a race-car driver?
If he had become a race car driver, the world might never have had 'Star Wars.'

CINEMA
1 STAR WARS

A Letter to George Lucas
Here is a fan letter to George Lucas. The parts of the letter have been labeled, and there are some grammatical mistakes. Use the proofreading marks below to edit the mistakes.

| ∧ Add text | ⊙ Add a period | ∧ Add a question mark |
| ≡ Capitalize letter | ✄ Take out | ✓ Spelling error |

Mr. George Lucas ← Heading
Lucasfilm
1110 Gorgas Avenue
San Francisco, CA 94129

Dear Mr. Lucas, ← Greeting

I love your movies! I like all six of them, but my favorite is *Attack of the Clones*. it was cool how Padmé, Obi-Wan, and anakin fight the arena creatures. I also liked how the clone troopers helped the Jedi.
I heard you are making three new movies. Will those be about Luke Skywalker I can't wait to see them.

Sincerely, ← Closing

Cary (age 10) ← Signature

A Letter From You
Would you like to write a letter to George Lucas?
Write a first draft of it here.

_____
_____
_____
_____

Now proofread your letter to make sure you haven't made any mistakes.
Use the checklist at right to make sure!

☐ Are all the words spelled correctly?
☐ Are paragraphs indented?
☐ Does every sentence begin with a capital letter?
☐ Does every sentence end with a period or a question mark?
☐ Are names capitalized?
☐ Do you have a heading, greeting, body, closing, and signature?

The sentences below are all highlighted in the article. Put a check mark by the meaning that fits the underlined word in each sentence.

Luke craves adventure.
☒ wants ☐ hates

The droids lead Luke to Obi-Wan Kenobi, a wise, old hermit living in the desert.
☒ thoughtful ☐ friend

Vader was once a pupil of Obi-Wan Kenobi, who had trained him to become a Jedi Knight.
☐ teacher ☒ student

Now Vader uses his Force powers for evil on behalf of the Empire.
☐ on half of ☒ on the side of

Will the Rebel Alliance defeat the Empire?
☒ beat ☐ lose to

Draw a line from the vocabulary words used in the article (in the blue boxes) to the words that mean the same thing (in the yellow boxes).

plot — story line
remote — distant, hard to get to
quest — a search for, hunt
evil — bad
thrilling — exciting, fun

Write a sentence for each of the words.

All About Lightsabers
Read the **essay** about lightsabers. Then answer the questions.

LIGHTSABERS

The favorite weapons of both the Jedi and the Sith, lightsabers are extremely powerful—but only in the hands of those who know how to use them! With blades made of pure energy, they can cut through anything (except another lightsaber).
Most Jedi have blue- or green-bladed lightsabers.* Jedi construct their own lightsabers from crystals they collect on Ilum, a mountainous ice planet. The lightsaber hilt is a complicated piece of machinery (see chart at right). Every Jedi designs his or her own lightsaber to suit his or her needs.
The Sith also make their own lightsabers. They are always red because they use the dark side of the Force.

Energy blade
Blade projection
Focusing crystal activator
Blade modulation circuitry
Handgrip
Handgrip chips
Blade length adjuster
Power insulator
Power cell
Pommel cap
Recharge socket
Radiator coating segment

*Footnote: *Mace Windu's lightsaber is an exception to this. His lightsaber is purple because of his unique connection with the Force.*

Answer the questions about the essay on lightsabers.

What is the main idea of this essay?
The main idea is to tell about lightsabers, including who uses them, what they are made of, and what the colors mean.

What color lightsabers do Sith have? Why?
The Sith have red lightsabers because they use the dark side of the Force.

What is the only thing that lightsabers cannot cut through?
They cannot cut through other lightsabers.

What is the footnote about?
It is about Mace Windu's lightsaber.

Look at the chart. What is the black button on the lightsaber called?
It is the blade length adjuster.

Answers

Answer the questions about the origami lightsaber instructions.

In Step 3, the instructions tell you to fold and unfold in half "lengthwise." What does "lengthwise" mean?

a) along the long part of the paper
b) diagonally
c) left to right

What step in the instructions tells when to turn the paper over?

Step 5 tells when to turn the paper over.

After following the instructions for step 7, the model

will turn into a ___triangular___ tube.

How many lightsabers were you able to fold?

_____

Start with this side facing you. Start with this side facing you. Start with this side facing you. Start with this side facing you.

Time to Alphabetize

Write all the words in the column on the left in **alphabetical order** on the right.

hermit	attack
sincerely	character
train	detests
footnote	diagonal
purple	essay
essay	footnote
diagonal	hermit
attack	purple
character	quest
detests	sincerely
quest	train

Choose any two words and use them in a sentence.

_____
_____

Answer the questions about the galactic timeline.

The timeline begins with what major event?
Anakin Skywalker is born.

In 4 ABY, whose life did Darth Vader save?
Darth Vader saves Luke Skywalker's life.

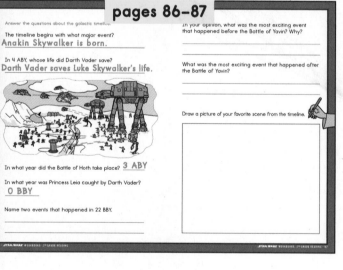

In what year did the Battle of Hoth take place? 3 ABY

In what year was Princess Leia caught by Darth Vader?
0 BBY

Name two events that happened in 22 BBY.
_____

In your opinion, what was the most exciting event that happened before the Battle of Yavin? Why?

_____
_____

What was the most exciting event that happened after the Battle of Yavin?

_____
_____

Draw a picture of your favorite scene from the timeline.